THE SACRED ADVENTURE

El Morya

RECORDED BY
MARK L. PROPHET

Library of Congress Catalog Card Number: 81-85464
International Standard Book Number: 0-916766-53-5

Printed in the United States of America
First Printing: December, 1981
Second Printing: April, 1982

This book is set in 10 point Century Schoolbook
with 3 points of lead.

Summit University 🝁 Press®
Los Angeles

To Lovers of

God's Will

Who Perceive

in Him

His Sacred Adventure

in Their Bodies

and in Their Souls

The will of God

Is the flawless diamond,

It is the shining

Of the Divine Mind,

It is the rushing

Of the wind of the Spirit,

And it is the strength

And laughter

Of real identity.

CONTENTS

PROLOGUE
SEVEN-LEAGUE BOOTS

*To the
Warriors
of Peace*

THE CENSURE of carnal minds, leveled by the children of men against one another, is an accumulation of deceit that is practiced upon the self and fostered upon an unsuspecting humanity.

The world may not take note of the treachery of mental viciousness, but like a Chinese torture chamber the human mind often seeks new inventions to bring pain and peril to the tenderest of hearts.

The affair in Czechoslovakia is just one more episode in a long line of infamous tyrannies to which the human race seems prone to fall heir. I shall not weary you with a long list of aggressions.

The prologues of world history, buried in

dusty mausoleums, are the sad mementos of a dingy past. Let us now set forth to examine a future that shall be based not upon the near past but upon the Beginning and upon the thoughts of the Ancient of Days.

Let us examine anew the ideologies of the Spirit. Let us seek votaries among men who will extend the domain of the divine thought through themselves, ennobling the mind of man and raising him Godward.

There is a force in the world that is not benign. It has sought to wreak destruction upon men by magnifying their supposed worthlessness.

We would show men their worthfulness and extend the best possibilities into the domain of the present hour.

Little do the kind ones dream of how the fruit of their kindness is dispersed and scattered abroad. The good seed falls upon the fallow ground the world around, and the fruit can often be traced to the most obscure sources.

We speak of the framing of beginnings, of the destinies of the fathers, and of the present hour as an extension of mercy into a future replete with gracefulness.

As we ponder the sky in the blueness of its color, we take note of the sapphire order, of the blueness that gemlike reflects the will of God. Whereas one knows that it is blue, one also knows that the white light has produced the fragrance of its appearance.

So is everyone that is born of the Spirit.

Those who are born of the Spirit have a tendency to exude the fragrance of mercy and hope. They open the gateways of the mind to the flood tides of divine resources.

They stimulate with gladness the flow of the fruit of goodness and mercy.

They thrust evil from them until it goes back into its lair, and in dauntless courage they sometimes follow it to a smashing retreat, soiling their garments in the hope of vanquishing it into a state of permanent rest.

Yet the hour has come when the signs of the wearing out of the world order do appear.

The mercies of the brothers of light, in considering in mercy's name a dispensation that would provide an extension of time before the Dark Cycle,[1] is commendable. The purpose of such a dispensation would be to prevent the destruction of useful, social instruments and to preserve order among men.

We embrace the will of God that,

working through the brothers of light, extends mercy to the uttermost. Yet as it has been said, "My spirit shall not always strive with man, for he also is flesh. . . . The grass withereth, the flower fadeth: but the word of our God shall stand for ever."[2]

We are concerned, then, with the Spirit that makes the bones fat, with the Spirit that extends the grandeur of cosmic architecture into the finite world, with the capturing in the net of Matter of some reflected glory of cosmic energy, with the accumulation of passions for hope, for beauty, and even for compassion.

The dire forebodings and ominous rumblings in nature and in man and the vicious openings into the astral currents that have been invoked by dabblers in black magic and dangerous drugs have brought about new maladies of the spirit, syndromes of praetorial decay producing lese majesty and permeating the world.

The legions of men are becoming neither more Godlike nor more manlike. They are simply dissolving their resemblance to reality in a chaotic nihilism.

We draw these analogies momentarily as we prepare to plunge into the fountain of reality in order that, by the startling power of contrast, we may show the world the true appearance of cosmic regeneration, of cosmic wholeness, of the washing of our garments white in streams of Cosmic Christ energy.

One of the problems of these times relates to the awful tirades of man against man. These ragings come from the mouths of evil spirits, speaking through embodied men and creating tortuous roadways where shadows obscure the path and detour the soul from its appointed round.

Now Morya speaks.

Beginning next week, it is my hope to strike a blow for God in the world order, to create a new series of teachings on the will of God—an offering based on such dedication and hope for an enlightened humanity as are the Great Divine Director's "Mechanization Concept," beloved Serapis Bey's "Dossier on the Ascension," and beloved Jesus' and Kuthumi's "Corona Class Lessons."[3]

As you know, down through the centuries men have discussed the will of God as though it were a thing apart from the will of man, bearing no resemblance to an offering that affords the best gifts to man. Contrary to human opinion, the will of God seeks to vest man with his immortal birthright and never to deprive him of his freedom.

Therefore, by his grace I shall show to the men and women of this age what the will of God really *is,* how it may be known, and how mankind may cooperate with it and use it as a means of extending the person (the pure son) into immortal realms.

We shall run the field if necessary. We shall request seven-league boots. We shall restimulate the fires of the Spirit in the chelas.

And, above all, we shall turn men to God because there is no other way whereby the soul can find the answer to all of its many problems.

The enigma of life is hidden within the will of God. When properly understood, it provides a stimulus for every worthy purpose and re-creates a passion for living that many have lost.

What you call zest or sparkle when

imbued with the Holy Spirit is no chimera but a flash of joy that ripples across the belly of the world, that sways the tallest pines and moves all things toward cosmic usefulness and cosmic purpose.

Some may wonder why I have chosen to speak. Now that the earth has entered the cusp of an age that is not innocent, I am impelled by the Great Divine Director himself, by the Prince of the House of Rakoczy, to seek to steal from the folds of the world those who have ears to hear that I may feed the sheep of God and safely shepherd them into the House of God's Will.

There is no other course to be run. But if there were, we should seek it.

This one has so many blessed avenues of service, so much greatness to offer to men that it is with relish that I elect to pursue the path of bringing once again to the world a greater understanding of the will of cosmic purpose—the will of God.

It will enhance my service to all men and to yourselves immeasurably if you will pray for me as I begin to intone those holy mantrams that will invoke in the sacred temples of the world, of the Great White Brotherhood, a refiring of the flame of God as we seek to reflect it—not only in words, but also in Spirit.

Adoring Him, I remain

El Morya

THE
GIFT OF
HIS WILL

*To Those
Who Seek
the Blue Heaven
in Which the
Sun Shines*

CHERISH: word symbol of arms clasped to the heart, the closeness of Reality, the beginning and the end of a search.

This is the will of God.

Seek, and ye shall find.[1]

Lessons are learned, and they are ignored. The journey of life, the long flow of identity, is a flurry of beginnings so separated from the Beginning that, in the farthest turn of the wheel, the beginning of the cycle is forgotten.

We raise the curtain of solar identity. We raise the cosmic curtain upon the mystery of life.

What is this ray flashing forth, this splendid, shining, far-off world? It is the will of God, permeating like a magnetic field. Yet the whole substance of cosmos is seldom sensed and seldom known.

In order to understand the earliest beginnings, it is necessary for man to consider the will of God.

The divine will sought to create, and create he did a majestic and finalizing plan for the beautiful unfoldment of the soul in the knowledge of the created self. And with the plan was given the means for the creation to keep pace with his own transcendent nature.

God sought to bestow, and the best gift that he could give was the gift of his will. For by his will he framed the far-off worlds, and by his will he sustained the momentum of life within each cell.

And so he heard the melody of the divine will. Some call it the music of the spheres, others perceive it in the faces of humanity.

Some cognize it in the revelations of science, others in the kingdoms of nature, while still others realize it in cloister. Retreating from the world, they hear it in the measured flow of the hours, in service, and in prayer.

All have heard it, but all have not recognized it. Only the few are able to see that which glistens like whitecaps upon the waves.

The tormenting substance of human drivel has opaqued the magnificent face of God that man can look upon but once and ne'er live as man again.[2]

Through this obscuration of the perfectionment of God, men are caught in the snares of their own choosing (or in those that are thrust upon them), in the strands of ignorance they have woven, and in the carelessness of treasured moments that slip so easily through the fingers of time.

What is this evanescent light? What is this courtesy of the givingness of God, of the holy will, and of the fire of the Divine Mother's heart?

How do you separate the will of God from him? Is his will a separate gratuity, an element of his grace which he gives to man? And if so, why does man not know it?

Does man know in part and sense in part the holy will of God? If so, what derision is it that seeks to mock the will?

It is the witless sophistry of sense meandering. It is the desire to rebel against the fashion of real beauty. It is the sense of separation and shame.

The will of God is the flawless diamond, it is the shining of the Divine Mind, it is the rushing of the wind of the Spirit, and it is the strength and laughter of real identity.

The will of God that seems so simple a thing is the most complex organism in the universe. From it sprang full-blown the entire scheme of cosmos, worlds without end—circles, pinwheels, spiral nebulae in cosmos, and the whole sidereal sea, all glowing fire-gems responding to the ministrations of the divine will.

Yet its cadences, like those of the melodic songs of a child, come forth with the simple beauty that adds meaning to each hour.

"How remote it all seems," you say.

Astronauts journeying out into space sense all of this immensity, but they cannot receive it within themselves; for they, too, have limited their consciousness. The dish of thought which they have made their portion is too finite and too small, albeit

9

more vast by far than that of ordinary men in their narrow frame of reference.

But now we seek to understand the thrust of purpose, to define the universe within the microcosm, man, and to relate the two through the extension of the Divine Will, the Divine Wisdom, and the Divine Presence.

For we cannot fail to gain some perspective of worlds within and without through His allness that brings to men the blessing of happiness and stops the simpering idiocy of thoughtless, witless minds.

And when the mind has grasped the principle of kindness and compassion, this tiny facet of the divine will can turn the lever of nations and cause them to respond.

What a miracle, then, is the will of God. And what is its fashion? It betrays no man, but summons the elect to the primacy of purpose.

What shall we say, then, to the careless ones who demand their own definitions and their definitions of definitions?

We will say with God, "I AM *Āgam,* the Unknowable. I AM the Infinite within who, in all of your winnings, can never be contained within the consciousness of sense or of perception."

Therefore the law of Love would bestow upon man the means to contact and to know the will of God.

It is an inward sense
We must discover and impart,
It is an inward sense
That rends the veil before we start.
We must convey our love to him
Who gives to us the grace to win,
The power to see the flow of truth,

11

The sweetest comfort, eternal youth,
And mighty power of light to live—
This is the radiance God does give.
In kindred minds he will impart
The holy will of God to start
The process over once again.

And thus we show that the will of God is
a seed to be planted within the consciousness of the individual, that the will of God is
substance, even as faith is,[3] and that the
will of God is the conglomerate stream of
reality—the issuance of purpose from the
uncreated realm into the realm of the
created essence.

I AM the beginning
And the ending of all things,
Of joy and beauty,
Of perfection and loveliness,
Of the strength and sweetness
Of the right arm of God.

The Gift of His Will

I AM the will of God,
The firmness of a cosmos
  that cannot turn
In response to tyrant's cry,
But flashes forth its light
Of mystery to meet the eye
Of mariner, ancient, bold,
Who seeks the way to fashion
Be it told—
I AM the will of God.
And so this will is right within
His Presence where you are,
And when you see it
Its fiery light will be a star
To open wide the chamber
Where the Real You lives.

Gratefully, I AM

El Morya

THE
INVIOLATE
WILL OF GOD

*To the
Sincere Ones*

VARIANCE creates disturbance. Variance is the stones of change. Variance is the disturbing stones thrown in the pond.

Waves of thought and feeling prevent the true reflection of the Real. Life does not mirror the will of God but in its place reveals distressing conditions.

One can control only the mind of self and the feelings of self, but one should ever remember that in a universe throbbing with the pulsations of the will of God the victors are many and their vibratory actions should be recognized.

Many peer instead at the myopic gray ones whose environmental concepts amplify the discord generated from or projected into their own worlds.

Morya speaks. We advocate the amplification of the will of God, for "the will of God is good."

The affirmation of this childlike statement over and over again is the means whereby the mind can be stilled and the mounting crescendo of human emotions diminished.

The will of God is the thunder of universal love. It is the strength of the right arm of the Almighty. It is the fire of his devotion and the best gift to his children.

There is safety in it and the strength that fashions security for the ages and beyond.

The *manvantaras* and the *pralayas*[1] may go forth, but those who cognize the will of God as the first vibration of his magnificent love will not be moved by the chirping of crickets, the boom of cannon, or the threatening ones.

Fear assaults the will of God, but the calm knowing of infinite love shatters the opaqueing conditions that scream from the minds of the depraved.

How long can they endure without the fire of the holy will? They steal light and energy, for they have lost their own. The children of the sun are their innocent victims, but not for aye.

Now come the wise ones. These are the peacemakers that are called blessed.[2] These are the children of God who understand the strength of the holy will.

In the Great Forever, in the beginning-ness of all things, God saw light and he was light. Out of his light went forth the beauty of loving purpose, and in him was no darkness at all[3] nor could there be darkness there.

This was the inviolate will of God—the same yesterday, today, and forever.[4]

The knowledge of good and evil, of duality, of the temporal and opposing factions that were within the range of the free will of the person—these came forth first as possibility and then as the looming shadows of karmic violation and disobedience to good will.

The tenets of brotherhood were clearly stated in the golden rule, "Do unto others as you would have them do unto you."[5]

But each violation produced its correspondent blot, its stain upon the page, and the Lords of Karma spoke: "This departure from the law of Good is but a repetition of the voices sent forth unto discord."

But there was an overthrust, a compulsion of the will of God, that sought to teach by the chastening of the law, thus to avoid the repetition of error.

The necessity of the will of God was clear. But while perfect love casts out all fear, for fear has torment,[6] what should be done for the impoverished ones, those who had lost their perfect love from the beginningness of God?

"Let them at least," said the Great Ones, "understand that God chastens those whom he loves,[7] and that he continues to love out of the bounty of his forgivingness."

Thus the will of God toward forgiveness was born in the consciousness of man. It was a step toward the regaining of perfection; for as men understood that as they had sowed so should they reap,[8] a desire to have perfection arose within them.

This desire to return to perfection through grace became the second corollary of the will of God.

Now the children of men who had erred saw the need to correct the error of their ways and thus be restored to the old boundaries of perfection—the perfection of perfect love.

The children of the sun, who came forth bearing the white stones from the Temple of the Sun, evoked the mightiest response possible from the hearts of men; for in the hearts of men there was also a residual memory of the olden days when the elder race communed with the living God.

Forgivingness, they saw, was eternal grace and the fire of purpose. Forgiveness, too, was the will of God. Thus the desire to return to perfect love flashed forth anew.

"Consider the lilies of the field; they toil not, neither spin...."[9] The cadences of the Master's words were dripping with

24

the fires of that perfect love that is his perfect will.

It is necessary that we establish in consciousness the concept of origins, for the majority of men's thought processes are patterned after the swing of the mind—to and fro.

This pendulum motion, often stemming from the restlessness of men's emotions, is part of mankind's struggle for that identity which has already been bestowed upon them.

But such movement can only swing men away from the peace of God and from his love.

Let men who would discover the will of God realize that it is already a part of the universe; that the universe, in the macrocosmic sense, is already the perfection of God; and that each star, each cell, and each atom was stamped with the divine image.

The words "Thou shalt have no other gods before me"[10] show the necessity for the Godhead to counteract the travesty of man's acceptance of fiats of imperfection. These have been issued by lesser minds and by the deceitful ones who are self-deceived.

The will of God that is good is naturally good. This goodness is inherent within nature, within the mind of man, and within all systems that were created by God in the beginning and which he sent forth to do their perfect work.

"Be ye therefore perfect, even as your heavenly Father is perfect."[11]

The desire for perfection is a natural manifestation of a perfect God shining behind his perfect manifestation, but all that which proceeds out of imperfection is against the divine nature.

The will of God is a security beyond belief, beyond faith, and even beyond manifestation, for it is the solemnly beautiful beaming of the tenderness of the Father's care for his creation.

Left undisturbed and permitted to express the elements of their cosmic identity, individuals would see themselves leaping into the arms of perfect love—the perfect love of God.

And the flashing of their divine identity would enable them to overcome all of those elements of the appearance world that have for so long distressed them.

And so the dream, the "impossible" dream, becomes the reality. And all that man has thought to be real, insofar as his own relationship with the universe goes, is seen as a chimera—a shimmering illusion that comes from misqualified energy.

In its place, in the place of the mirage of carnal identity with its shifting sands of manifestation, the reality of the Christ identity is seen as the will of God.

What difference does it make that there are opposing forces?

The forces of Light are more dominant, the forces of Light are greater, the forces of Light are complete and eternal. They will stand when men are but dust and their present thoughts hollow echoes in the chambers of memory.

Let men understand that it is not the Father's will that they should perish but that they should have abundant life.[12]

When we begin to examine the great thoughts of God and the great will of God, when we begin to examine how great God is, we must see that cardinal to his

greatness is the abundant life, the life
that is eternal.

It is fear—fear of death and fear of
illusion—that has caused some men to fail
to hold themselves in that state of consciousness wherein the will of God could
manifest through them.

They need to understand the very natu-
ralness of cosmic purpose: God is life.

They are manifesting temporal life, but
they also possess, here and now, the seeds of
eternal life in the very essence of the soul
which God has given to them.

The flaming Presence that directs them
from above, their beloved God Presence,
"I AM,"[13] represents the fire of the will of
God; and the will of God includes within
itself the all-chemistry of cosmic purpose.
Therefore, each department of life is
brought under the direction of the central

purpose of the will of God.

What folly it is that individuals feel separated from the will of God, as if they could not know it! For his will begins in the simplicity of a child and in the simplicities of nature.

It is so natural and sweet that in their sophistication men often lose its tenets. The pathway to regaining it is the pathway the Master Jesus taught: "Verily I say unto you, except ye become as a little child, ye cannot enter in." [14]

The result of becoming as a little child is rebirth, a being "born again" [15] into the consciousness of the kingdom of heaven.

And I assure you that the will of God will teach you to expand your being until from the tiniest little seed, like unto a grain of mustard seed, [16] you shall become a tree of cosmic purpose identifying with the divine will.

What thundering concepts are captured within the simple ideas of faith, hope, and charity!

Forward we move into the ever-expanding light.

Your elder brother, I AM

El Morya

"HOW CAN I KNOW THE WILL OF GOD?"

To the
Builders
Who Seek
Truth

HOW CAN I know the will of God?" This is the cry of millions.

Man presupposes that the divine will is hiding from him, as though it were a part of the plan for the Eternal God to play hide-and-seek with him.

Not so! The will of God is inherent within life and merely awaits the signal of release from man's will in order to ray forth the power of dominion to the world of the individual.

There is a sovereign link between the mortal will and the Immortal. In the statement of Jesus "It is the Father's good pleasure to give you the kingdom,"[1] men can be aware of the eternal will as the fullest measure of eternal love.

Release, then, your feelings of possessiveness over your own life! Surrender the mean sense of sin and rebellion, the pitiful will to self-privilege which engenders bondage.

See the will of God as omnipresent and complete, the holy beat of the Sacred Heart throbbing within your own.

Know and understand that surrender is not oblivion but a point of beginning and of greater joy.

Now responsibility does not cease but begins anew, and man is yoked with eternal purpose—the shield of God's will.

O how joyous is the touch of thy hand,
O living flame.
How comforting this contact
By night or day.
We are not alone anywhere,
For thy presence is a succoring shield.

"How Can I Know the Will of God?"

"Dominus vobiscum"* to all substance
And the infusion of the Spirit of Hope
In the purposes of men
As they blend most tenderly
Into the purposes of God.
Through surrender
The molding process can begin.
Waves of cosmic energy
With or without conscious awareness
Literally flood body, mind, and soul
With strength of purpose, defying inertia.
We live because thou livest in us.
We are in a state of consonance
   with thy purposes,
And O how glorious are those concepts
Of givingness to life!

The Great Giver is perceived
As the only true friend to us all—
Our common bond of brotherhood
   and strength.

---

*"The Lord be with you."

Allied with invisible legions,
The weld of strength and purpose
Becomes increasingly persistent.

Shelter me from delusion, O God,
To whom shall I fly?
For thy way is the best way.
Old residual habits seek banal
  reexpression.
To opaque the holy will is their purpose
And to excite me to evil strength
  and shame.
Yet short-lived are the carnal
  creature comforts,
And dark is the desiring of mortal
  wayfaring.

The sheltering arms of thy will
  come again,
And I AM known of thee
Even as I increase my knowledge
  of thy will.

"How Can I Know the Will of God?"

Down through the ages I have known
   many names,
Thou hast known but one name,
The strength of thy arm is my salvation,
The joy of my heart,
The solitary consoling factor of life,
The joy of my desiring
And the manifesting of thy light,
My purposed will!

By doing, by identifying,
By just becoming aware of thee
I automatically know thy will.
Increment by increment
I AM adding to the perfect knowledge
That casts out the fear of oblivion
And gives my soul the peace thou hast
Because my mind is stayed on thee.

Strength, strength, strength be multiplied,
And love, be thou increased!
All these are found in the holy will.

Born out of increased devotion,
They take their own full measure
Of action and renewal.

Long has the soul been dead
In the night of personal delusion—
The struggles, the accumulated
    karmic debts,
And the great harms.
Now the end has come
In one solemn sweet surrender:
I AM—Thou art—we are—
All are One!

Yet the finite span,
The temporal shafts of darkness
Remain a blight and pit
    to snare the soul.
Can my resolve to *be* thy will in action
Be a shield so strong
That never again shall submit
    to carnal will
And the pitfalls of the senses?

"How Can I Know the Will of God?"

The body cries out in pain,
The mind does reel in anguish
Of human condemnation.
These are not thy will
But only that the soul
   should gain in light
And bask in the willing of thy love.

What peace is mine that dares
   not be afraid
To seek the depths, the heights,
The riches of thy soul?
The soul of God is one great sea of promise,
Interconnecting all with all that lives.
Yea, saint and sinner of all ages past
Do rise or fall in him.

All life does live or perish
   in his memory vast
And does return to him complete
   or yet unborn,
Unfinished by his grace.

Our souls are torn by splendor
Contrast 'gainst the night.
A higher purpose and a holier will
   are born,
We seek and find new light
   with coming morn.

O not my will, my will be done
   but thine.[2]
Great drops of blood betray my anguish—
Thine the glory and the power, Lord,
Thine the kingdom shining
O'er the hills of time
Revealing, as we upward climb,
The starry ladder of thy grace.
As angels to and fro do go,[3]
Our souls do know thy purpose dear.
And in communion, strength appears
As triumph over death.

Morya cries out, O weary traveler, know him ere it is too late!

So many tempt God one more time, fearing they may miss some passing earthly joy.

The will of God is an interpenetrating essence that flows through substance, mind, and motion, conveying new images and changing old ones into transcendence. To die to all of this marvelous flow of living light by closeting the soul in vain desire is an abomination beyond terror.

Come out now, then, and see the sole goal of eternity shining through the strands of time. What a marvelous gilding of opportunity is to be found in the pursuit of his will. And it can be known!

We cringe for a distraught humanity, caught up in the passing paradise of the senses.

Man's inhumanity to man is not destroyed by a liberal sense, neither is utopia secured by developing a sense of social justice or an outreach toward world betterment which denies immortality.

Only by union with God's will can the world, one and all, come to peace and perfection in a relative sense, stretching toward the good things to come that spring forth in eternal life.

How myopic are the "savers" who store their world's goods like camels in little humps of survival and are themselves utterly barren of soul substance. The will of God is the will of change for man that feeds the flame of life within and changes mortality into immortality.

It would seem that what the senses cannot report is unbelievable unto many, and yet the life that beats the heart of man is not seen or known by any save the few.

Many wonder how man, made in the image of God, could have fallen so low. Let them realize that deteriorations occur first in consciousness.

Hence, when men indulge in simple flights of imagery that are not in keeping with divine ideals, they take the first steps in departing from the will of God. A downhill course is more difficult of reversal than an ascendant one.

We evoke the consciousness of God in our disciples, for in God's own thoughts the alchemy of change is wrought. Men are not realists when they mull over the murky patterns of human history.

The distortions of life recorded on the strata of mortal consciousness are full of arson, murder, and debauchery. Strangely enough, justification of these crimes by individuals sometimes causes them to become imbued with a sense of righteousness as though they did God service.

The topsy-turvy attitudes of such folly prove why men are wont to change light into darkness and darkness into light.

The will of God is purely beneficial to all the earth, yet wholly tethered to the infinite love of the Father without human favor or distortion.

Now we call for the clear seeing of the God consciousness in all life as the first step toward immaculate victory which all must take if they are to be reborn in the divine image and likeness.

The quality of thoroughness in all things men do weds them to a sense of the immaculate and the perfect; but herein men must exercise care, lest false pride in accomplishment give rise to a spirit of criticism of others whose outer care for perfectionment remains yet undeveloped.

The Father's attitude of reflecting only pure love and communion with all who desire to manifest this love is the exemplary mode which all should follow.

This *satsanga,* or "fellowship with truth," is the invisible coming together of the body of God upon earth in one real cosmic brotherhood that can never deny its likeness to the heavenly will.

Does shallowness of being mean that man can never become full of grace and the manifestation of God's will? I say, nay. For if the vessel be shallow, enlarge it; if the substance be minute, increase it!

God's will is everywhere manifest, but it must be sought and gathered. The substance of things hoped for and the evidence of things not yet seen[4] must be held as potential for all.

In the fullness of faith in the divine creation, men must identify with the hidden man of the heart[5] and out of this oneness they will roll up victory after victory right in the teeth of seeming defeat.

Knowing the longing and the hunger of the souls of men for the real, I am diligently evoking the symbols of his will to manifest in you as alertness of mind, willingness to change, and the courage to offer the self of mortality to the lovely designs of the Father's purpose.

The Brotherhood cannot be affected by mortal doings, but human life can!

We urge that faith be implemented by right action and that the confidence of each student in his personal relationship with the God Presence as the repository of God's will be upheld.

"How Can I Know the Will of God?"

Thus shall the finite line be extended and the eternal 'try-angle' be perceived as the setting for the calm eye of cosmic vision to survey all things and direct all things by the plumb line of everlasting justice and mercy.

I AM the Master Mason, directing the pyramid of lives to the summit of attainment.

Graciously, I AM

El Morya

THE
OWNERSHIP
OF GOD'S WILL

Precious Seekers

CREATE unto yourself the new sense of the ownership of God's will!

You have long thought of God's will as a thing apart from yourself. Now, new longings and a fresh perspective can re-create the best gift you have ever had.

The memory of his grace can come alive within you as you accept the infinite care of the Eternal One for you. His blessed consideration of your lifestream must be contemplated and made a living, vital part of your whole consciousness.

For far too long man has yielded his birthright unto the false, the insecure, and the transitory. But when he pauses to think of his source, there should come to mind the best gifts of life—the ever-present thought-fulness of God about his rate of progress, his advancement, his endowment, his protection, and his ultimate fulfillment.

Why, God can be made so central, so real, and so intimate to the very being of any man who diligently seeks his will (tutoring both inwardly and without) that he will scarcely remember his former state of unbelief!

It merely awaits an opening, a twinkling of the eye of being, for the last trump of immortality to sound and to change the lesser image into his glorious divine reality![1] This can be, for it already *is!*

Why do men set up a counterfeit will and call it their own? Why do they engage in a continual struggle between the will of God and "their own" will? In the answers to these questions is to be found the key to happiness for every part of life.

When man understands that there is no
need to struggle for a personal existence
outside of God (because he is complete in
God) and that, in actuality, there are not
two wills—the will of man and the will of
God[2]—but only the will of truth and freedom, inherent within the very Spirit of Life
which is the Spirit of God, then he will
enter into the new sense of harmony and
grace.

Every man should realize his essential
individuality, his privilege God-given of
expressing unique qualities of life that he
can use to endow the universe from the
fountain of his own life and love.

But, there are lessons to be learned,
understandings to be sought and found,
and old senses to be cast aside, transmuted
and, in some cases, re-created.

Morya thunders! Why should we put off the hour of the emptying of the mind of its delusions? Why should darkness impel the mind and heart to distrust themselves?

Let us infire men with a gnosis of possibilities. Let us create a sense of strength based not upon weakness but rooted in the flow of reality. The fact that men have not known does not mean that ignorance should continue.

We send light on the holy will and it permeates the consciousness, bridging the old gaps and steaming the spirit loose from its confining walls where the insidious glue of human consciousness has dried up the very thought of progress.

Sultry spirits infest the gullible and the complacent! We speak to those who are willing to be God-willed!

The Ownership of God's Will

The very idea of "me" and "mine" often leads to separation. The strange consciousness of schism finds welcome wherever men love darkness.

They ply the boat of consciousness into watery caves of intricate folly. But the clarity of the will of God promotes the facility of smoothened reality.

Now the Word long ago went forth, but the common man skulks in fear lest someone should find out that he is in league with God or the holy will!

Shames are honored while the source of all grace remains hidden in shame from puny mortal eyes. Truly, the blind lead the blind.[3]

Walk ye in the dominant way of the sacred stranger who respects no man's illegitimate thoughts but every man's person (pure son).

The counting of the hours is good when worth appears. Yet the hairs of the hour's head are numbered.[4] Finite screens frame eternal possibilities.

Change, blessed change, how beloved thou art! Yet for thine own sake, let us make clear that only the turning to the awful noontide of truth will show the scorpion on the ground.

Alertness spares man the spawn of infectious evil and hallows the blessedness of Christ expansion. The meaning of the incarnation is not measured in hours, but in events!

The wayfarer lingers too long at the stagnant pool when the glories of the fragrant moment are near. Every moment spent in learning to live in the will of God is a blessed one.

The sense consciousness may not glow in

the will until it has developed its spiritual appetite (for good), but *akasha*[5] will record each benevolent thought and action to the expansion of cosmic grace in the obedient ones.

The will of God is the sole source of man's freedom.

For many, unlearning is more vital than learning. The science of the soul can be mastered by the soul without any effort save sweet surrender, yet the education of the heart will school the whole man in the understanding of amazing dimensions.

"Where have these realms been all my life?" men will cry. Where indeed but right where they are, resident within the heart of truth.

The will of God is known only by the very few; for many who think they have this precious commodity are clinging to the vine of mortal reason, opinion, and a whinnying whimsy!

I think, then, that reappraisals must be made and that they should be based on the vein of God's mind and not upon sense criteria. Why should men not ask that they may receive, seek to find, and expect the descent of radiant grace?

The world is often fooled by those who proclaim longevity on the Path. Little do they know the compounds of the Eternal Chemist who, in the laboratory of nature, has also created subtleties to satisfy the natives of aeons!

Where away? Certainly we must flee the present.

Ever in the dim as well as in the near past have we thought upon the escape from the contemporary net, from the hypnotic trap of the manipulators, through the freshness of sound vision.

But peripatetic visions[6] must be eschewed. Men must ask of God grace to discern the higher will as the bright threads of hope, implemented by practical action and endowing the heart with the leap of boundlessness.

So dear is the will of God to me that if I had to take upon myself a body once again and descend into form here, I would willingly do so for the sake of God's will.

Alas, this cannot be. And I must satisfy myself to look downward from these glorious realms of light in the hope that men and women taught the three R's and the sweet homilies of human life will, as many of us have done, espouse these eternal causes.

May they do so diligently in order that the Great Magnet will be successful in drawing the flame within the heart into magnificent attunement, raising the whole body of mankind's consciousness into the blessed light of the holy will!

In one very real sense the links with heaven are so beautifully woven that if men could see them clearly in all of their blazing reality, they would need no other polestar upon which to fix their gaze as an escape to eternal hope.

Yet the carnal welds men have synthesized are so tenacious as to defy perfection, and they bind men embodiment after embodiment in the old oily schemes of selfishness that shrivel the soul in the carnal will.

What can we do but hold forth the vision of the grail of God's will as the beacon of every hour.

Along with the vision of personal

ownership of God's will, one should also think upon the omnipresence of the will.

Darkness thickens in the carnal mind;[7] simultaneously, the light dazzles the consciousness with nearness. To draw nigh unto the light: this is the requirement of the hour!

The flashing forth of the renewal of the first covenant is the will of God; for it was this bond to which every soul who received the gift of individual life expression did once consent.

The breaking of the bond of God's will has meant the parting of the way between father and son. For the prodigal son has chosen to wander into the depths of maya to seek his fortune in the realm of illusion.[8]

Now we say, let us return to reality, to the Father, and to the heavenly will.

Thus shall the fire purify each man's work[9]
and the fiery trial cease in a pact of friend-
ship with God.

Victoriously, I AM

El Morya

"NOT MY WILL, BUT THINE BE DONE!"

*To All
Wanderers
of the
Spirit*

THE FIRST flush of freedom, how magnificent! Now, no longer engaged in a sense of struggle, man becomes a part of the holy sea ("And before the throne there was a sea of glass like unto crystal. . . ."[1]).

The will of God, how clear and lovely—a beautiful dream filled with no thoughts of the human nightmare. The promise "My grace is sufficient for thee"[2] becomes a tangible reality as man is enclosed within the strength of God's will.

When the hymn "A Mighty Fortress Is Our God"[3] was released, it was to be a tribute to the divine will; and I think there is no greater goal for any man than to identify totally with this universal lifewave of cosmic creativity.

Yet many do fear to surrender their own will to the universal. They fear to lose their identity when in reality they would but "loose" their identity and find it again in the blessed sense of self-direction that exists in higher octaves of harmony.[4]

For harmony is a divine sense, an afflatus of such vibrancy, buoyancy, and oneness with all life that heaven can never imagine how anyone who has tasted thereof can ever again return to the soil of carnal expression.

Children of the cross, awake and see how you can benefit men by bestowing upon them the prime example of your godly accomplishments for and on behalf of the light!

The need is great. And it is God's will that we gather the children of the sun under the canopy of the divine radiance!

Men have accused me of hardness. Let me tell you, there are two kinds of hardness: (1) hardness of heart, which is wholly selfish and wedded to pride and ambition, that never says die to its Moloch of self,[5] and (2) the hardness that identifies with the diamond of good will—God's will for total good, total intelligence, and total opportunity.

The latter, in its grand design, is the simplicity of the crystal that reflects the passion of the soul to live within the protective love of the Father without compromise to other expressions.

This is the diamond of perfection that incorporates the quality of mercy and gives balance without straining at a gnat or swallowing a camel![6]

There are so many forms of subtlety in

use upon earth today that the process of knowing the will of God is at times difficult.

For example, some conceive of poverty as being the will of God; these make their lives an example of total simplicity. Others see opulence and abundant supply as the will of God.

In reality, neither state can guarantee victory to the soul but rather the gift of nonattachment which can either use the empire of the universe in all its fullness or be content in any environment.

The truly illumined are able to rise above states of mind or expression to the place where they identify with the allness of God.

In the early church, the controversy arose between those who ate meat and those who did not.[7] Saint Paul advised that the true believer should condemn neither attitude, for Jesus had said, "Not that

which goeth into the mouth defileth a man;
but that which cometh out of the mouth,
this defileth a man."[8]

How important it is, then, that men do
not judge at all lest they be judged.[9] For
those who live in poverty as well as those
who are surrounded by the greatest wealth
can be doing the will of God. To his own
master each one stands or falls.

The enemy in the guise of good, in a
subtle form of criticism, purports to
describe just what qualities and conditions
will prove the existence of a so-called
master. This may lead those who follow
such an outline of what masters supposedly
"do" and "don't" into the banal pathway of
criticism.

Those who go about examining "masters" to see if they are following the "rules"
may enter the same spirit of condemnation

which is apparent in those well-meaning teachings that appear benign but are based upon false standards of condemnation and judgment.

Let all understand that, even as our palace of light in Darjeeling does reflect all of the grandeur and more of a maharaja's palace, God does not forbid his son to partake of his abundance. For these blessings are within the latitude of cosmic privilege.

They are earned by the soul who knows that all things come from God and that they are to be used to bless life abundantly: "For whosoever hath, to him shall be given, and he shall have more abundance: but whosoever hath not, from him shall be taken away even that he hath."[10]

Yet to the spiritually rich and to the spiritually poor I say, your life is not in the material, but in the spiritual. However, when total surrender to God is made, all things can be safely added unto you.[11]

It is more blessed to give than to receive; but if you do not first receive, may I ask, how can you give?

Therefore, it is the Father's good pleasure[12] to endow you with his Spirit and also with material substance whenever the Lords of Karma see that benefits to humanity can be released through your blessed lifestream.

The will of God is everything. For it provides the spark that pushes back the darkness of sense consciousness, of ignorance and despair while holding forth the torch of true illumination to the seeking soul, enabling each individual to find himself, lost in the passion of God's will!

Can you now understand how I, when embodied as Sir Thomas More, did see beyond the tower cell and loss of life and did reach outward to uphold principle for that age, fully confident of my identity in God?

Yet those who betrayed me within a few short years did leave the old familiar scenes for regions of nether nonsense. Truly, men who build in the holy will do build for eternity!

Be wise, then, in the simplicity of God. Be content not to judge men but rather to inspire them to that coagency of marvelous reality: the will of God.

Blest be the tie that firmly binds that holy link. For when men do otherwise, seeking in their own way to express the vagaries of the human will, a vain expression of whimsy and discontent is always the outcome.

The will of God is not so, for it represents

the original archetypal thought of God that identifies uniquely with the soul of the individual. Holding ties with universal man, it maintains its own personal vital unity.

Like a refreshing breath of pine, the ideas of God fill the air with a raising hope that destroys the personal illusion while bestowing the real crown of Life upon victorious man.

In heaven's name, men of earth, do you think the Most High God created life to manifest as history shows it?

And what of contemporary struggles twixt church and state, race and race, class and class, and even man and man or man and woman?

Does life seem so wonderful and the prospect of the future based on human trends so grand that you are fearful of submission to the will of the Eternal?

I hope not, for in his will is comfort and strength for the ages as well as for today.

The fiat "Not my will, but thine, be done"[13] was not intended as a statement of sacrifice but one of heavenly inspired wisdom. In the higher schools, this mantram of the Spirit is intoned invocatively so as to create the needed liaison between man and God.

Whereas it is God's will that man intune with him, it is incumbent upon man to recognize that his responsibility demands search, willingness, and an understanding of the self-created barriers that must be taken down so that the clarity of the will of God can come through.

The reason that the releases of the Brotherhood in the Pearls of Wisdom[14] are slanted to different levels of human thought and expression, offering invaluable

82

advice to mankind, is so that these Jericho-like walls of opposition to your union with God's will can be broken down.

Little keys unlock the biggest doors, and man must be ready to walk through and not stand hesitatingly upon the threshold.

You will never know how indecision or vacillation can alter the mind to turn a deaf ear to the voice of God. That is why it was once wisely said, "He who hesitates is lost."

Be ready mentally, spiritually, and emotionally by an act of simple devotion or a feeling of awe to accept the will of God as a gladiator would a laurel wreath.

Eras of achievement lie ahead—the planning of great cities, civilizations, and humanitarian doings. But until the will of God becomes acceptable to men, until they can put aside their double-mindedness, they will remain unstable and fluctuating in their aims. [15]

The terrors of their world exist first in their denial of God and secondly in their denial of his will. In order for the kingdom of God to manifest upon earth, it must first manifest in the heavenly consciousness.

Let men think heaven and think God's will, let them deny the power of darkness and the light of holy knowledge will show science and religion the way to happiness through finite days to infinite aeons of bliss for all.

Thus God ordained it, thus man must seek to know!

O holy will, descend to earth we pray,

El Morya

THE
HUMAN WILL

*To Our
Very Dear
Aspirants*

of what the will of God is, therefore they do not really know what they are opposing.

The human will opposes the divine will because its aims are shortsighted. Men find it difficult to expand their thought beyond their days. They are prone to accept death as final and to identify with the physical form rather than with the spirit which gives it life.[2]

That there is a very definite interest in the afterlife is witnessed by the large number of people who speculate on and profess to believe in survival after death.

It might interest them to know that from the viewpoint of the Spirit, when man is born he is considered to have died. The reason for this is that spiritual substance possesses the quality of malleability, whereas on earth centuries are sometimes required even for the construction of a cathedral.

For example, when men begin to build a large building they first complete the architectural design and then proceed to build the physical structure.

But in spiritual realms men can actually create the blueprint of an idea in their minds and then release it into manifestation almost with the speed of light. Like some of your modern electronic computers, the sum appears upon the screen almost as fast as the keys are punched.

There is a reason why manifestation in the lower octaves is slowed down. It is in order to give people an opportunity to dedicate themselves to higher values and to avoid the mistakes associated with haste.

If carnal man were permitted to precipitate his will with the speed of light, the cruelty that would follow would be incomprehensible. Man's containment within a framework of natural law has provided a safety valve against the accidental destruction of all civilization.

Wise men have thought upon this and they have conceded that with the present use of atomic energy, world destruction could become inevitable.

Certainly, it behooves mankind en masse to understand the need to guard the educational channels of the world; for succeeding generations can easily have their attitudes altered, as they have had in the last three decades, to such a point that standards of morality and decency, upheld since man's emergence from the Dark Ages, will be trampled upon and lost.

Whether or not a recovery can now be made quickly enough to preserve civilization is a problem for both man and God. Hereditary and environmental influences may be strong, but environmental influences can in a short time eradicate centuries of right living. Of course, I speak in a relative sense.

Would it not be wise then for man, caught in the net of illusion, to examine the purposes of God, to know them, to understand and serve these mighty purposes in order to accelerate in his own personal evolution the divine plan and to foster the architecture of heaven for all mankind?

The problem of absolutes is always at hand—absolute Evil and absolute Good. These conditions are so remote from the average person that their concern lies not in the absolute but in the relative.

They are concerned not with the question "Is it a condition that manifests good or evil?" but when making a moral decision they ask, "Is it relatively good or evil by comparison to other conditions, and does it represent the best choice?"

Understanding moral values, which are valid because they are based on truth, will help men to understand that their progress must come from their present state and move forward. Too many are obsessed with the idea of a utopian ideal which, because it is unobtainable, they use as an excuse for lowered standards.

The law of the circle exacts its full toll: what men do unto others they receive unto themselves.[3] The way to success, to prosperity, and to happiness is to give happiness unto others.

The simplicities of the Master's way have been made plain in the midst of a complex civilization. The pathway of the Spirit that is so childlike and sweet is in any age wondrous to live when verified by the Spirit of truth within oneself.

Cultivate, then, the Spirit of truth.[4] Invite an honest analysis of situations.

This will not require hours of your time when it is evoked out of an honest heart. The will of God that has already engraven his wisdom and love upon your heart will enable you to draw reasonable standards toward which you may reach.

God will not seem so remote nor his will when men are able to envision it as an extension of their own consciousness from present standards to those that are still higher.

But when men consider their own standards to be above the stars, then like an animalistic cult they grunt and groan, dance in circles, and dissipate their energies in vanity.

We are concerned that the will of God

come into fuller manifestation in the world of men. But in a relative sense, one man's idea of the will of God may be a far lower standard than it is for another.

Men must realize that some have higher standards than others and that some can attain higher goals. Life is not meant to be filled with criticism and condemnation, but it is an opportunity to thwart the human ego which must ultimately reflect God if it is to endure.

This is the real purpose of the existence of man: to reflect God and then to identify with the Real Image that is reflected within.

To improve the quality of the reflecting mirror is essential; in this way consciousness itself, as a chalice, can be improved so as to contain, not only qualitatively but also quantitatively, more of the will of God.

If individuals would just grasp the principle that the will has been hidden from them, that over the centuries they have seen only remote flashes reflected in the cup of life and that these flashes are responsible for all of the betterment of humanity, they will understand that the will of God is the panacea of healing for the world order as well as for the individual.

Conversely, they will recognize that the will of man, tethered to no sense of the real but following its own darkened star, can never lead to the Promised Land or give man his freedom and permanent place in the universal scheme.

From time to time, the Brotherhood releases buoyant ideas—sometimes simple, sometimes complex—into the minds of the students. These ideas are not always assimilated immediately. Albeit instant love is the will of God, it is not always the possibility of man.

Therefore, these teachings on the will of God are given in order to re-create in consciousness certain engrams* that will enable you to accomplish effectively and by consent your release from the carnal mind and to replace it by the buoyancy of the mind of God.

As a little Father, I remain in your service,

El Morya

---

*Engram: a geometric formula of the Word that manifests as a forcefield of light.

A
SACRED
ADVENTURE

Eternal Seekers

IN THE BEGINNING God created the heaven and the earth. And the earth was without form, and void; and darkness was upon the face of the deep. And the Spirit of God moved upon the face of the waters."[1]

It is to this point that we would return in order to reveal the tenderness of the eternal will, for the light shone in the darkness and the darkness comprehended it not.[2]

It is, then, to comprehension that we dedicate our closing release in this series on the will of God.

Thought is buoyant, but whose thought is more buoyant—man's or God's? If man thinks God's thoughts, are they ineffective because he is man?

The affection of the will is its raison d'être. A will without affection is a non-entity. The natural affection of God for the creation is apparent within the creation, for the fire of creation is the affection of the will of God.

The ability to affect Matter and Spirit simultaneously is the prerogative of the divine will which, in a lower harmonic range, is observed in part by evolving men.

The laws of containment which govern time cycles and the enlargement of space involve the spreading apart of divine ideas from the center point unto the circumference of manifestation.

The tenderness of divine love refuses to yield itself to a moment of sympathy; for such indulgence would deny immortal opportunities, and it is even questionable that it would satisfy temporary thirst. Yet the mercy of the law is functional and practical, and man is never deprived of grace by submission to the will of God.

The grace that is sufficient for every day[3] is extracted from the universe by an act of will when that will concerns itself with glorifying God through outer manifestation and purpose.

The will of man is not capable of expanding self or substance, but dedication to the supreme purpose invokes the will that moves mountains.

Man can do the will of God without knowing it, but by being conscious of himself as a part of the will of God he is able to fulfill his destiny in a more sublime way.

The talents and opportunities of life are given to man as stepping-stones toward spiritual achievement, and spiritual achievement is the only goal that is real, hence worthwhile. Eternal life can best be enjoyed spiritually, for "flesh and blood cannot inherit the kingdom of God."[4]

The form maker, who is the form breaker, can also be the form remaker. No loss can occur when one serves the eternal will, for the revelation of the will of God shows the seeker the abundant face of reality.

One glimpse has been sufficient for many avatars who were thereby exalted out of the socket of contemporary worldliness into positions of universal service and love.

The greatest boon comes to those who surrender willingly with or without understanding, but always in the confidence of a faith that observes the universe and its myriad wonders and grasps with the simplicity of a child the reality of universal science.

Known by any name, God is still the

Creator-Father of all life and his will bears the fashion of acceptance by all of the emissaries of heaven.

Every active power by which the universe is sustained and managed in the light of cosmic justice comes forth from him, and every spirit that he has created returns to him.

Each spirit is intended to be made like unto him, hence in his image. Any lesser dominion is the having of "other gods before me."[5]

Therefore, the holy will appears as the fullness of the swaddling garment of the Divine Man, the Son of Righteousness, with which the children of the sun must be clothed.

Stand now to release thyself from the darkness that is in thee[6] and face the luminous orb of the Central Sun from whence all creation sprang.

Mindful of his will for good and of his power to extend that will, realize that he is able to extend thy consciousness from its present state—to pick it up, to exalt it, and to draw it into himself by the magnetism of his grace—here and now, prior to thy release from sense consciousness.

Realize that he that keepeth all that *is real*[7] about thee, having received thee momentarily unto himself, is also able to return thee to the present moment unaffected adversely but mightily affected inwardly by a fuller measure of the understanding of his will.

Realize that the will of God can best be known by a spiritual experience. Desire, then, that experience. Desire to reach outwardly toward the Godhead in the Great Central Sun galaxy.

At the same time as thou art reaching inwardly to the implanting of the divine seed within thyself, it is the will to live within thyself that must unite with the will to live as God lives.

This is the divine will within the heart of the Central Sun. This thou must understand and be united with.

If this be accomplished but once consciously, thy life shall ever thereafter be affected by an innate knowing, recorded within, of that which is the will of God. The phantoms and the ghosts that formerly made thee a stranger at the court of heaven will no longer hold power over thee as they once did.

But man's reunion with the Sun can only be accomplished by an act of God. It is a cosmic event which can occur in the world of the individual only when he has proven himself ready for it.

I am a cosmic teacher, and I choose to appear to those who are able to see me with their spiritual eyes, to those who understand that my prime concern is the union of the heart of hearts within man with the Heart of Hearts within God.

For me to provide descriptive passages of these wonders and to record them on paper would in no way compare to the glorious experience that can occur as you rise through the trackless air and far-flung reaches of space into a realization of the will of God that penetrates all substance and all nature.

You must be able to go deeply within, for not in outer accouterments of name or fame or even in worldly intellect does man find the keys that will transport him to these higher reaches.

We caution that great care must be exercised in this matter, for truly we are not concerned with the developing in men and women of untutored or unguided psychic experience. We want this form of communion to be a rarity rather than a daily practice.

It is something one should try no more often than once a year in just this manner, with the exception of those who have been mightily prepared by advanced training. For them there will unfold the necessary direction which will assist them in having vital experiences to guide them in their solar evolution.

You must understand that the will of God is a sacred adventure.

I have said it thusly for a reason, for the average individual considers an encounter with the will of God a remote possibility.

He prays to have the will of God made known to him, but he does not understand that he can have an a priori glimpse of that will while yet in mortal form.

He does not realize that the will that sees can also be seized, in part, as a treasure-house of consciousness and carried back into the domain of the life within. There the great lodestone of truth acts as a divine revelator to reveal to each man from deep within his own heart what the will of God really is.

Above all, let him understand always that, complex and all-embracing though it may be, the will of God can always be reduced to the common denominator of love, life, and light.

Forward we go together.

I AM simply, your

Morya

NOTES

Introduction

1. The Dark Cycle of the return of mankind's karma began on April 23, 1969. It is a period when mankind's misqualified energy (i.e., their returning negative karma), held in abeyance for centuries under the great mercy of the Law, is released for balance according to the cycles of cosmic Law in this period of transition into the Aquarian age.

2. Gen. 6:3; Isa. 40:8.

3. See the Great Divine Director, "The Mechanization Concept," in *Pearls of Wisdom*, vol. 8, pp. 9–142, or *The Soulless One*; Serapis Bey, *Dossier on the Ascension: The Story of the Soul's Acceleration into Higher Consciousness on the Path of Initiation* (Los Angeles: Summit University Press).

Chapter 1

1. Matt. 7:7.

2. Exod. 33:20.

3. Heb. 11:1.

Chapter 2

1. Epochs of cosmic history.

2. Matt. 5:9.

3. I John 1:5.

4. Heb. 13:8.

5. Luke 6:31.

6. I John 4:18.

7. Prov. 3:11, 12; Heb. 12:5, 6.

8. Gal. 6:7.

9. Matt. 6:28.

10. Exod. 20:3.

11. Matt. 5:48.

12. Matt. 18:14; John 10:10.

13. "I AM": the name of God given to Moses, I AM THAT I AM (Exod. 3:13–15). The "I AM Presence" is that portion of selfhood which is the permanent atom of being; the Monad of self suspended in the planes of Spirit just above the physical form; the Godhead individualized

115

as a living flame, a point of consciousness, a sphere of identity.

14. Matt. 18:3.
15. John 3:3.
16. Matt. 13:31, 32.

Chapter 3

1. Luke 12:32.
2. Luke 22:42.
3. Gen. 28:12.
4. Heb. 11:1.
5. I Pet. 3:3, 4.

Chapter 4

1. I Cor. 15:52.
2. Saint Paul called the will of man "the law of sin" which was in his members (in his consciousness). He recognized the presence within himself of a power apart from God, and he knew that as long as he permitted this force to remain in the inn of his being, it would war against the "law of his mind" or the will of God. He also said,

"Where the Spirit of the Lord is, there is liberty," showing that when one disarms himself of all opposition to God and seeks the very presence of his Spirit as the only reality, then he is free from all lesser manifestations. (Rom. 7:23; II Cor. 3:17)

3. Matt. 15:14.
4. Matt. 10:30.
5. *akasha:* primary substance; the subtlest, supersensuous, ethereal substance which fills the whole of space. Energy vibrating at a certain frequency so as to absorb, or record, all of the impressions of life. These recordings can be read by those whose soul faculties are developed.
6. Here the master references philosophical meanderings and speculations which are not based upon the laws of God.
7. Rom. 8:6, 7.
8. Luke 15:11–32.
9. I Cor. 3:13.

116

Notes

Chapter 5

1. Rev. 4:6.
2. II Cor. 12:9.
3. "A mighty Fortress is our God, / A Bulwark never failing; / Our Helper He amid the flood / Of mortal ills prevailing: / For still our ancient Foe / Doth seek to work us woe; / His craft and power are great, / And, armed with cruel hate, / On earth is not his equal. . . ." Words and music by Martin Luther.
4. John 11:44.
5. Mark 3:5; 16:14; Rom. 2:5.
6. Matt. 23:24.
7. Rom. 14; I Cor. 8.
8. Matt. 15:11.
9. Matt. 7:1.
10. Matt. 13:12.
11. Matt. 6:33.
12. Luke 12:32.
13. Luke 22:42.
14. Pearls of Wisdom are weekly letters of instruction dictated by the ascended masters to their chelas throughout the world through the Messengers Mark and Elizabeth Prophet. Free Pearls of Wisdom are sent weekly throughout the U.S.A. for a minimum love offering of $33 per year. Write The Summit Lighthouse, Box A, Malibu, CA 90265.
15. James 1:8.

Chapter 6

1. John 14:1; Matt. 19:26.
2. II Cor. 3:6.
3. Luke 6:31.
4. John 14:16, 17; 15:26; 16:13; I John 4:6.

Chapter 7

1. Gen. 1:1, 2.
2. John 1:5.
3. II Cor. 12:9.
4. I Cor. 15:50.
5. Gen. 1:26, 27; Exod. 20:3.
6. Matt. 6:22, 23.
7. Pss. 121:4.

INDEX

Abomination, 45

Absolutes, the problem of, 94

Abundance: God does not forbid his son to partake of his, 78; "...and he shall have more abundance...," 78. *See also* Abundant life; Prosperity; Rich; Supply; Wealth

Abundant life, 28; as the life that is eternal, 29. *See also* Abundance

Accomplishment(s): pride in, 48; your godly, 74. *See also* Achievement; Success; Victory

Achievement: eras of, 83; spiritual, 107. *See also* Accomplishment(s)

Action: faith implemented by right, 50;

practical, 65. *See also* Doings; Motion; Work

Adventure, the will of God is a sacred, 113

Advice, invaluable, 82-83. *See also* Direction

Affection, 106. *See also* Love

Afterlife, 91. *See also* Eternal life

Āgam, 11

Age, that is not innocent, *xix. See also* Dark Ages; Eras

Aims: passing, 89; shortsighted, 91; unstable and fluctuating, 83-84. *See also* Goal(s); Purpose(s)

Akasha, 63

Alchemy, of change, 47. *See also* All-chemistry

Alertness: of mind, 50; spares man the spawn

strength as triumph over, 44; survival after, 91. *See also* Dead

Decay, syndromes of praetorial, *xv-xvi*. *See also* Deteriorations

Deceit, an accumulation of, *xi*

Deceived, self-, 26. *See also* Delusion

Decency, standards of, 93

Defeat, victory in the teeth of seeming, 50

Definitions, 11

Delusion(s): the emptying of the mind of, 60; the night of personal, 42. *See also* Deceived

Depraved, the minds of the, 21

Desire, vain, 45. *See also* Ambition

Despair, 79

Destiny, 107. *See also* Divine plan

Destruction, world, 93

Deteriorations, occur first in consciousness, 47. *See also* Decay

Devotion, an act of simple, 83. *See also* Love

Diamond: the flawless, 8; of good will, 75; of perfection, 75. *See also* Gems

Dimensions, the understanding of amazing, 63. *See also* Realms

Direction: necessary, 113; self-direction that exists in higher octaves, 74. *See also* Advice

Discontent, 80

Discord, 19; voices sent forth unto, 22

Disobedience, to good will, 22

Dispensation, *xiv*

Divine nature, imperfection is against the, 26-27

Divine plan, 94. *See*

Index